Abingdon's

SPEECHES & recitations for YOUNG children

🔔 Abingdon Press

CONTENTS

GOD IS IN THIS HOLY TEMPLE

God is in this holy temple;
On this holy Sabbath Day,
Let us praise God, Let us thank God,
As we worship, sing and pray.

God is in this holy temple;
Knowing all we do and say,
May our service and our offerings
Honor God this Sabbath day.

—Ida F. Leyda
(adapted)

WELCOME TO OUR SUNDAY SCHOOL

Welcome to our Sunday School,
On this holy, happy day;
Gladly will we share with you
All the things we do and say,
For we love to greet you here,
And we hope you'll want to stay.

—Ida F. Leyda

A CHILD'S OFFERING

The wise may bring their learning,
  The rich may bring their wealth,
And some may bring their greatness,
   And some bring strength and health;
We, too, would bring our treasures
  To offer to the King;
We have no wealth or learning:
   What shall we children bring?

We'll bring Him hearts that love Him;
   We'll bring Him thankful praise,
And young souls meekly striving
  To walk in holy ways:
And these shall be the treasures
  We offer to the King,
And these are gifts that even
   The poorest child may bring.

We'll bring the little duties
  We have to do each day;
We'll try our best to please Him,
  At home, at school, at play:
And better are these treasures
  To offer to our King,
Than richest gifts without them;
   Yet these a child may bring.

—The Book of Praise for Children, 1881

6

ALL THE HAPPY CHILDREN

All the happy children
    Thank you, Lord above
For this day for children,
    And for your great love.

We will still remember
    We are yours alone;
For the one who made the summer
    Made us every one.

Frances Bent Dillingham (adapted)

HEAR THE GENTLE SHEPHERD

Hear the gentle Shepherd
Calling lambs like me
In the sweetest accents,
"Let them come to me."

He will bid us enter,
When our tired feet
Reach the golden city,
He'll be there to greet.

Thanks dear blessed Jesus,
For your words of love,
Bidding children enter
Your bright courts above.

—A. H. Adams

GOD IS NEAR

(First child)
>Sometimes when morning lights the sky
>And gladness fills the air,
>I feel like telling things to God,
>He seems so very near.

(Second child)
>Sometimes when flowers are in bloom
>And birds are singing clear,
>I feel like singing things to God,
>He must be very near.

(Third child)
>Sometimes when trees are standing tall
>With branches in the air,
>I feel like saying things to God,
>I know He must be near.

(Fourth child)
>Sometimes when work and play are done
>And evening stars appear,
>I feel like whispering things to God,
>He is so very near.

—Elizabeth McE. Shields
Copyright 1927 Elizabeth McE. Shields
Used by permission.

BIRDS SINGING IN THE TREETOPS

(First child)
> Birds singing in the tree tops,
> Flowers blooming in the grass,
> Close by the shady pathways,
> Where children love to pass.

(Second child)
> Clouds floating high above us,
> Boats sailing out to sea,
> Far from the sandy seashore,
> Where children love to be.

(Third child)
> Hill, mountain, field and valley,
> Each one in beauty dressed;
> And all the spreading shade-trees,
> Where children love to rest.

(All)
> These all make happy summer,
> God's gift—the great outdoors;
> He made the trees and flowers,
> The sea and sandy shores.

—Ida F. Leyda

DO YOU KNOW WHO MADE THE NIGHT?

(First child)

> Do you know who made the night?
> Made the stars and moon so bright?

(All)

> God our Father made the night,
> Made the stars and moon so bright;
> Our Father made the night.

(Second child)

> Do you know who made the day?
> Made the glad and happy day?

(All)

> God our Father made the day.
> Made the glad and happy day.
> Our Father made the day.

(Third child)

> Do you know who made the trees?
> Waving gently in the breeze?

(All)

> God our Father made the trees,
> Waving gently in the breeze:
> Our Father made the trees.

LONG AGO THE LITTLE CHILDREN

Long ago the little children
Gathered close at Jesus' knee,
For His kindly smile said gently,
"I love them and they love Me."

Come and listen to the story,
Friend of children still is He;
Listen then and whisper softly,
"I love Him and He loves me."

—*Jesse Eleanor Moore*

FOR THE FUN OF SINGING

It's such fun to sing a song,
To sing the music sweet and long;
While we go about our play
It keeps us happy all the day!
Because you put these happy songs
Within our hearts where joy belongs
We thank you, loving Lord!

—*Arletta Christman Harvey*

JESUS HEARS

(For an older child)

Jesus hears me when I pray,
Listens to the things I say;
Knows the feelings deep inside
That I sometimes want to hide.

Jesus tells me, "It's okay,
Many people feel this way.
Come and tell me all your cares.
I will listen to your prayers."

—*Jackie Wilson*

MY DAILY CREED

(First child)   Let me be a little kinder,
        Let me be a little blinder
    To the faults of those about me;
        Let me praise a little more;
    Let me be, when I am weary
        Just a little bit more cheery;
    Let me serve a little better
        Those that I am striving for.

(Second child)   Let me be a little braver
        When temptation bids me waver;
    Let me strive a little harder
        to be all that I should be;
    Let me be a little meeker
        With someone who is weaker;
    Let me think more of my neighbor
        And a little less of me.

—Anonymous

NATURE'S CREED

I believe in the brook as it wanders
    From hillside into glade;

I believe in the breeze as it whispers
    When evening's shadows fade.

I believe in the roar of the river
    As it dashes from high cascade;

I believe in the cry of the tempest
    'Mid the thunder's cannonade.

I believe in the flash of lightning,
    I believe in the night-bird's croon.

I believe in the faith of the flowers,
    I believe in the rock and sod,

For in all of these appeareth clear
    The handiwork of God.

—Anonymous

GOD'S PROMISE

(First child)
> God made the rainbow,
> So pretty to see.
> This beautiful gift
> Is God's promise to me.

(Second child)
> Every time thunder
> And lightning appear,
> I think of the rainbow
> And know God is near.

(Third child)
> God will not leave me
> Alone anywhere.
> No matter what happens,
> I know God is there.

—Jackie Wilson

EVER THANKFUL

> Ever thankful
> I will be,
> To my God who
> Cares for me.

> Resting safely
> In God's care,
> I know that God
> Is always there.

—Jackie Wilson

WE ARE SPECIAL

God the Father
Loves me true.
God the Father
Loves you, too.

God loves each of
Us the same.
Even knows us
By our name.

We are special
In God's sight.
God made each of us just right!

—Jackie Wilson

GOD'S GIFTS

God gave us hands
To touch and feel;
Loving hands
To help and heal.

God gave us arms
To reach and hold;
Arms to circle
And enfold.

God gave us hearts
Filled with love and care;
Not to keep,
But to give and share.

—Jackie Wilson

WHY GOD MADE THE STARS

God put the stars
In the sky
Up above the
Earth so high.

Made them twinkle,
Shine and glow;
Beaming love to
All below.

God sent Jesus
Down to earth,
To show the world
How much we're worth.

—Jackie Wilson

FOLLOWING GOD'S WORD

Little kids are very great
According to the Lord.
They can do 'most anything
By following God's word.

—Jackie Wilson

FEELINGS

I have a feeling
You can't see,
A feeling deep
Inside of me.

It's so big I
Can't begin
To tell you where
It starts and ends.

It bubbles up
And overflows—
This special feeling
Grows and grows.

What is this thing
Inside of me
That I can feel
But you can't see?

Let me tell you
What I know.
It comes from God
Who loves me so.

God fills me up
From head to toe
With love and joy
Then tells me "Go

Tell my people
Everywhere
I love them, too
And really care."

—*Jackie Wilson*

GOD'S PRECIOUS LOVE

God's precious love
Is reaching out
To take away
All fear and doubt.

It's reaching deep
Inside our hearts
To show us we
Are each a part

Of God's great plan
To always be
God's children
Through eternity.　　*—Jackie Wilson*

GOD'S BLESSING

See the stars so shiny bright
Twinkling in the sky tonight.
Made by God so long ago
So that you and I can know;

God created everything,
Fish that swim and birds that sing.
God created you and me,
Made so all the world can see;

The special gifts
That we each have
To bless the world
On God's behalf.

So celebrate when
You see the stars,
The fish, and birds,
And know we are

God's special gift
Each and everyone,
To bring the blessings
Through Jesus, God's son.　　*—Jackie Wilson*

17

JESUS WALKS BESIDE ME

Jesus walks beside me,
He's with me every day,
Helps me with decisions
I make along the way.

He knows, when I see sorrow,
That my heart just wants to break.
Jesus wants to touch my heart
And all the sorrows take.

Jesus gives me courage
For things that I must do,
Fills me with the strength I need
To last my whole life through.

—Jackie Wilson

LIGHT OF LOVE

Light of love
Alive in me,
Brightly shine
So all can see.

Love of God
That's in my heart,
Precious love
Sets me apart.

Light of love
Alive in me,
Jesus shines
For all to see.

—Jackie Wilson

SUNDAY SCHOOL

(For one older child or four younger children.)
I like to come
To Sunday school
And sing the songs
So beautiful.

To worship God
In song and praise
And learn the truth
Of Jesus' ways.

I like to hear
The story told
Of God's pure love
Like shining gold.

I like to learn
Of Jesus' ways
To share with others
Everyday.   —*Jackie Wilson*

SUNDAY SCHOOL

(First child)   I love to come
To Sunday School
And learn about
The Golden Rule.

(Second child)   I listen as the Bible's read
And hear the words
That Jesus said.

(Third child)   Love the Lord your
God each day.
Love others too,
And learn to pray.   —*Jackie Wilson*

19

GOD'S LOVE

(First child)   Thunder rumbles
In the night.
Lightning flashes,
See the light!

(Second child)   God has spoken
Through the noise.
Listen, you will
Hear God's voice!

(Third child)   Softly rain drops
Start to fall,
God's own way of
Touching all.

(Fourth child)   Soon the summer
Storm is past.
Stars peek through
The clouds at last.

(Fifth child)   Twinkling down from
Up above,
Silently they
Speak God's love.

—*Jackie Wilson*

SHARING

God created you and me,
Gave us home and family,
Told us all we have to share
So that others know we care.

—*Jackie Wilson*

HELLO

(First child)   I just came to say "hello"
And brighten up your day,
To tell you you have a friend
Who wants to come and stay.

(Second child) Jesus wants to be your friend
Wherever you may go.
He wants to live inside your heart
His precious love to show.

—Jackie Wilson

THE LORD IS EVER NEAR

The Lord is ever near,
He bids all children pray;
While they are speaking God will hear,
And bless them day by day.

—Author Unknown

LORD, WHEN TO YOU A LITTLE LAD

Lord, when to you a little lad
Brought the small loaves of bread,
Your touch enlarged the gift until
Five thousand folks were fed.

So will you take our offerings small,
Of time, and work, and love,
And multiply them many times,
With blessings from above.

—Author Unknown
(Adapted)

COME UNTO ME

Jesus our Savior said,
Come unto me,
Children of every land,
My own to be.　　　*—Ida F. Leyda*

THE LITTLE CLOUD

Little cloud up in the sky,
Looking down as it goes by,
Sees the children at their play,
Then it sails far, far away,
Over land and over sea.

Little cloud sails through the air,
Sees the children everywhere;
Little faces sweet and bright,
Some are dark and some are light,
Over land and over sea.

Little cloud, please as you go,
Tell the children this is so:
Jesus Christ is God's own son,
And he loves them every one,
Over land and over sea.　　*—Ida F. Leyda*

A LOVE MESSAGE

I want to send a whisper song
Across the waters blue,
And say to all the children there,
Jesus Christ loves you.

If they should not understand,
They'll wonder if it's true;
But I will keep on whispering still,
Jesus Christ loves you.　　*—Author Unknown*

GOD'S GIFT OF WATER

Each little flower holds up its cup,
To catch the rain and dew;
The drink God gives to seeds and flowers
Is best for children, too.

The little bird fresh water drinks
And seems to love it too,
And then he raises up his head
As if to say, "Thank you."

God gives water to everything,
It makes life strong and new;
And for this gift of water pure,
The children thank God too.

—*Ida F. Leyda*

JESUS AND THE CHILDREN

(First child)

What did he say, who from above,
Came down to teach us kindness and love?

(All)

"Let the children come to me, for theirs is the
kingdom of heaven.

(Second child)

What did Jesus tenderly say,
When others wished to send us away?

(All)

"Let the children come to me, for theirs is the
kingdom of heaven."

23

MORNING AND EVENING

Every morning seems to say,
"There's something happy on the way,
And God sends love to you,
And God sends love to you."

Every evening seems to say,
"I am with you all the way,
And God sends rest to you.
And God sends rest to you."

—First verse, Henry Van Dyke
—Second verse, Ida F. Leyda

A SERVICE FOR RALLY DAY,
CHRISTIAN EDUCATION SUNDAY OR CHILDREN'S DAY

(Scriptures are paraphrased)

Quiet Music

Prayer

Recitation: *God is in This Holy Temple (5)*

LEADER: This is God's house. How should we enter God's house?

CHILDREN: Enter God's gates with thanksgiving, come into God's courts with praise.

LEADER: This is God's day.

CHILDREN: Remember the Sabbath day. Keep it holy.

LEADER: To whom do the days and nights belong?

CHILDREN: The day is God's and so is the night.

Recitation: *Morning and Evening (24)*

LEADER: God made day and night and everything in the world in which we live.

CHILDREN: In the beginning God created the heavens and the earth. *(Genesis 1:1 KJV)*

LEADER: What other things did God make?

CHILDREN: God made summer and winter. God made the sea and God's hands formed the dry land. God made everything. Nothing was made without God.

Recitation: *God's Blessing (17)*

LEADER: God is good to us, giving us this beautiful world, giving Jesus, our homes, our family and friends.

Recitation: *Sharing (20)*

LEADER: In what way may we tell of God's goodness to us?

Recitation: *Hello (21)*

LEADER: Is God's goodness for us alone?

Recitation: *Long Ago the Little Children (11)*

LEADER: When we say God is good to all, whom do we mean?

CHILDREN: All people everywhere.

LEADER: What invitation shows that Jesus loves all children?

CHILDREN: Let the little children come to me, for theirs is the Kingdom of Heaven.

LEADER: How can we help people everywhere know Jesus?

CHILDREN: By giving money to send missionaries and supplies. By sending the Bible, pictures, stories and songs. By asking God to make everything speak of Jesus and his love.

Recitation: *The Little Cloud (21)*

TEACHER: We have so much to make us thankful, because God has given so many good gifts.

Recitation: *Thank You, God (59)*

LEADER: Jesus loves to use children's gifts. A story in the Bible tells how he used a boy's gift to help many people.

Recitation: *Lord, when to You a Little Lad (21)*
Offering
Prayer: *Giving (60)*
Recitation: *Welcome to Our Sunday School (5)*
Recitation: *Parting Prayer (60)*

SNOW

Soft flakes of snow,
Like feathers blow,
God gives snow like wool;
Keeping seeds warm
From cold and harm,
God gives snow like wool.

—*Ida F. Leyda*

ADVENT

Advent candles
Light the way
For Christ to come
On Christmas day.

And we are very hopeful, too
Christ will come
One day for you.

—*Jackie Wilson*

CHRISTMAS WELCOME

Children dressed in
Shepherds clothes,
Angel wings, and
Gold halos,

Here to share
A story true
Of the gift God
Sent to you.

Welcome.

—*Jackie Wilson*

THE SHEPHERD SPEAKS

Out of the midnight sky a great dawn broke
And a Voice singing flooded us with song.
In David's city was He born, it sang,
A Saviour, Christ the Lord. Then while I sat
Shivering with the thrill of that great cry,
A mighty choir a-thousandfold more sweet
Suddenly sang "Glory to God, and Peace . . .
Peace on the earth;" my heart, almost unnerved
Speechless we waited till the accustomed night
Gave us no promise more of sweet surprise;
Then scrambling to our feet, without a word
We started through the fields to find the Child.

—John Erskine (1879)

TRIUMPH OF THE SEASON

Triumphant the season passes.
Rich and poor express goodwill
Gaining strength for days to follow
Warming hearts in Winter's chill.

As upon this Christmas morning
Gifts we open joyfully.
Let us understand God's presence
As we practice charity.

Christmas rings with jubilation
Of the Christ child whose creation
Channels peace and joy unfurled
All throughout the whole wide world.

—Merle Ray Beckwith

THE SHEPHERDS HAD AN ANGEL

(A reading for an older child)

The shepherds had an angel,
    The wise men had a star,
But what have I, a little child,
    To guide me home from far,
Where glad stars sing together,
    And singing angels are?

Lord Jesus is my Guardian,
    So I can nothing lack;
The lambs lie in His bosom
    Along life's dangerous track:
The wilful lambs that go astray
    He, bleeding, fetches back.

Those shepherds, through the lonely night
    Sat watching by their sheep,
Until they saw the heavenly host
    Who neither tire nor sleep,
All singing 'Glory, glory,'
    In festival they keep.

Christ watches me, His little lamb,
    Cares for me day and night,
That I may be His own in heaven:

    So angels clad in white
Shall sing their 'Glory, glory,'
    For my sake in the height.
Lord, bring me nearer day by day,
    Till I my voice unite,
And sing my 'Glory, glory,'
    With angels clad in white,
All 'Glory, glory,' given to Thee,
    Through all the heavenly height.

—Christina Georgina Rossetti

A GIFT FROM HEAVEN

Just a little baby,
Jesus was his name,
Bringing joy and gladness
When from heaven he came.

—*Ida F. Leyda*

CHRISTMAS

(For three older children and several younger)
(First child)

In another land and time,
Long ago and far away,
Was a little Baby born,

(All)

On the first glad Christmas day.

(Second child)

Words of truth and deeds of love,
Filled his life from day to day;
So that all the world was blest,

(All)

On the first glad Christmas day.

(Third child)

Little children did he love,
With a tender love always;
So should little children be

(All)

Always glad on Christmas day.

—*Ida F. Leyda*

ON THE HILLS OF JUDAH

(For three older children)

(First child)   'Twas on the hills of Judah,
One bright and starry night,
That shepherds heard the singing,
And saw the heavenly light.

(Second child)   It was the angel chorus,
The song from heaven above,
Telling the glad story
Of God's great gift of love.

(Third child)   For God so loved all people,
He gave His only Son,
To be a friend and helper,
And savior to each one.

—*Ida F. Leyda*

CHRISTMAS DAY

(First child)   Christmas day
Is the special way
We join God's celebration.

(Second child)   Of Jesus birth
Here on the earth
With praise and adoration.

(Third child)   Carols are sung
And garlands hung,
Through days of preparation.

(Fourth child)   Faces shine bright
As the candle light
Reflects God's love and devotion.

—*Jackie Wilson*

THE CHILDREN'S PLAY

I'd like to be an angel
In the Christmas play this year.
I said so at the tryouts
But nobody seemed to hear.

I tugged on Mother's shirtsleeve
As I squeezed her hand real tight.
"Please tell them that I want to be
An angel Christmas night."

I said a prayer to Jesus
Saying if it was Okay,
I'd like to be an angel
In the children's Christmas play.

Now here's what Jesus told me,
Softly whispered in my ear;
"I need a lot of children
To present the play each year.

The angels are important
For they tell of Jesus birth.
They bring the news from heaven
To the people down on Earth.

But every part's important
If my story's to be told,
Just the way it happened
Long ago in days of old.

So whether you're an angel
Or a wiseman from the east,
The mother at the manger,
Or a shepherd tending beasts,

By helping tell the story,
Playing any part with style,
To me you'll be an angel
With a halo and a smile." —*Jackie Wilson*

CHRISTMAS MORNING

(First child)   The sky can still remember
      The earliest Christmas morn,
When in the cold December
      The Savior Christ was born;

(Second child) And still in darkness clouded,
      And still in noonday light,
It feels its far depths crowded
      With angels fair and bright.

(Third child)   O never failing splendor!
      O never silent song!
Still keep the green earth tender,
      Still keep the gray earth strong;

(Fourth child) Still keep the brave earth dreaming
      Of deeds that shall be done,
While children's lives come streaming
      Like sunbeams from the sun.

—*Phillips Brooks*

THE STARS SHONE BRIGHT

(First child)
    The stars shone bright that Christmas night,
    When Jesus lay on His bed of hay.

(Second child)
    The shepherds came from far away
    To find the place where the baby lay.

(Third child)
    The wise men brought their gifts of love;
    Led by the star that shone above.

—*E. Webster*

HAPPY NEW YEAR

Happy New Year everyone!
Sing a song of praise.
Thank you God for giving us
Your gift of precious days.

—Jackie Wilson

NEW YEAR'S DAY

Angel voices sang last night
For all the world to hear.
Their tinkling voices rang like bells
To welcome God's New Year.

—Jackie Wilson

THE WISE MEN

Over hill, across the desert sand,
Slowly toward the Holy Land,
With them precious loving gifts of love they bring
Asking for the new-born King.

When they saw the Child they all rejoiced,
Worshiped him with tender voice,
Bowing low, presented gifts of love
To the Christ-child from above.

—Ida F. Leyda

LONG YEARS AGO

(First child)　　　　　Long years ago
　　　　　　　　　　　Wise men with joy
　　　　　　　　　　　Brought birthday gifts
　　　　　　　　　　　To a small boy.

(Second child)　　　　From the east they came,
　　　　　　　　　　　Thro' deserts wild.
　　　　　　　　　　　And they brought their best
　　　　　　　　　　　For a little child.

(Third child)　　　　　Long years have passed,
　　　　　　　　　　　And Christmas joys
　　　　　　　　　　　Fills the whole wide world
　　　　　　　　　　　For girls and boys.

—*M. Lanning Shane*

CHRISTMAS SERVICE

Music: O Holy Night

Prayer:

Recitation: *God is in This Holy Temple (5)*

LEADER: God's House, God's Day, God's Book tell about God and God's great love. What was God's greatest gift to us?

CHILDREN: For God so loved the world, that he gave his only begotten son. *(John 3:16 KJV)*

Recitation: *Christmas (30)*

LEADER: Long before Jesus came, just as a little baby, God had promised that some day he would send his Son. The people had waited and watched for many years, but it was to the shepherds out on the hills watching their sheep that God sent the message, "for unto you is born this day in the City of David a Savior."

Recitation: *The Hills of Judah (31)*

LEADER: But it was to Mary, the baby's mother, to whom God sent the message, by an angel, what his name should be.

Recitation: *A Gift from Heaven (30)*

LEADER: God wanted others to know about the baby Jesus. It was by a bright, glorious star that he sent the message to some wise men far, far in the east; that the savior of the world had come. They hastened to follow the star that they might present their gifts and worship him.

Recitation: *The Wise Men (34)*

LEADER: We wish all the children of the world knew the story as we do. But in some far away countries the children have never heard the name of Jesus, nor the story of the shepherds and the wise men. Jesus wants some one to tell them. Our Christmas offering will help some one to go tell them about Jesus.

Offering:

Recitation: *God in Heaven Bless All Children (60)*

SPRING SUNSHINE

God sends the sunshine
Warm and bright
To wake the earth
From Winter's night.

—*Jackie Wilson*

RAIN

Springtime showers
From up above,
Bring the flowers
That show God's love.

—*Jackie Wilson*

FLOWERS

Up pop the flowers
Through the ground
Open their petals
And look around.

Each little flower
Doing its part
To show the love
That's in God's heart.

—*Jackie Wilson*

HOW FLOWERS GROW

(First child)   First a seed so tiny,
Hidden from the sight;
Then two pretty leaflets
Struggling toward the light.

(Second child)

Soon a bud appearing
Turns into a flower,
Warmed by golden sunshine,
Washed by silver shower.

(Third child)

Growing sweeter, taller
Every happy hour!
Showing God's great kindness
And God's wonderful power.

—*Ida F. Leyda*

NATURE'S MESSAGE

(First child)

The little flowers peep through the ground
To say to people all around,
"Your heavenly Father sends his love
To you and you and you."

(Second child)

The birds come back each happy spring
To say to people as they sing,
"Your heavenly Father sends His love
To you and you and you."

(Third child)

The trees are dressed in gowns so new;
They say, "We have a message, too,
Your Heavenly Father sends His love
To you and you and you."

—*Elizabeth McE. Shields*
Copyright 1924 by Elizabeth McE. Shields
Used by permission.

'TIS GOD WHO SENDS THE SPRING

(First child)   I'm very glad the spring has come,
The sun shines out so bright;
The little birds upon the trees
Are singing with delight.

(Second child)   I love to see the pretty flowers
That rain and sunshine bring;
When all things seem just like myself,
So glad to see the spring.

(Third child)   God must be very good indeed
Who made each pretty thing;
For flowers and birds and sunshine say
"Tis God who sends the spring."   *—Ida F. Leyda*

EASTER WELCOME

Easter morning's
Here at last.
We've waited
For so long;

To celebrate
This special day
With worship
Praise and song.   *—Jackie Wilson*

AN EASTER PRAYER

God's blessing rest upon you
  This happy Easter Day,
God make His joy to shine
  As sunlight on your way;
God fill your heart with song
  So glad it will not cease;
God bless you every day
  With love and joy and peace.   *—Anonymous*

A THOUGHT

He who died on Calvary,
Died to ransom you and me.

On the cross He bowed His head,
In the grave He made His bed.

Ever since, the lilies bloom
Round the portal of the tomb.

Ever since, o'er all our loss.
Shines the glory of the cross.

—Margaret E. Sangster

EASTER

(First child)

Springtime tells of Easter glory,
Sweet and fair;
Easter bells ring out the story
Everywhere;

(All)

The Lord is risen!
The Lord is risen!

(Second child)

All the happy world rejoices,
Far and near;
Children sing with happy voices
Sweet and clear;

(All)

The Lord is risen!
The Lord is risen!

—Ida F. Leyda
(adapted)

BRIGHT EASTER DAY

(First child)   Mary's heart was
Filled with gloom
As she walked to
Jesus' tomb.

(Second child)   Missing Jesus
Christ her Lord,
Friend that she had
Long adored.

(Third child)   Jesus spoke to
Her and said,
"Mary, I'm no
Longer dead."

(Fourth child)   Mary ran to
Spread the word,
Sharing all she'd
Seen and heard,

(All)   To everyone along the way,
Christ our Lord is risen today!

—*Jackie Wilson*

AN EASTER PRAYER

I sing this happy prayer, Dear God,
For joy and Easter-time,
For birds that sing
And earth so fair,
For springtime beauty everywhere!

And I know why—for Jesus lives!
In all the world today
It's "waking time."
And glad hearts say,
"We thank you, God, for Easter day!"

—*Arletta Christman Harvey*

AN EASTER SERVICE

(This service could also be used any Sunday in the Spring.)

Quiet Music

Recitation: *Prayer (58)*

Song: *Holy, Holy, Holy*

LEADER: God's word, the Bible, tells many beautiful things about God, God's great love for us, and God's promise to us. What is God's promise about seedtime and harvest?

CHILDREN: While the earth remains, seedtime and harvest, and cold and heat, and summer and winter, and day and night will not end.

LEADER: God gave us winter with the happy Christmas time. Now as the days grow longer and warmer we know that spring will soon be here.

Recitation: *Nature's Message (38)*

LEADER: God sends the warm spring sunshine to make the grass grow, so that God's creatures may have food.

CHILDREN: You cause the grass to grow for cattle.

LEADER: God sends the warm spring rains to give drink to flowers and trees. The rain fills the streams and rivers. All of God's creatures find a place to drink. What Bible verse tells this?

CHILDREN: You give drink to every beast of the field.

LEADER: God's great gift of water is not only for birds and flowers and the creatures of the field, but for all God's children. Everything needs water; it brings new life. It is the best drink for all.

Recitation: *God's Gift of Water (23)*

LEADER: All of God's great gifts in the heavens above and in the earth below speak of God's goodness and power.

Recitation: *Nature's Creed (12)*

LEADER: A verse in the Bible tells us God is mightier than the mighty waves of the sea, and a story in the Bible tells of God's power to quiet the waves and the storm.

Recitation: *God's Love (20)*

LEADER: High mountains, deep ravines, the great wide fields make us think of God's love and power. Springtime and harvest, all seasons of the year, sun, moon, and stars, the wide sea, the splendid fields that God has given us make us want to say again

ALL: The earth is full of the goodness of the Lord.

LEADER: God makes little brown seeds change into flowers. God makes the dry, dead looking bulb grow into a lily. God makes the bare trees to be covered with leaves. God gives new life to the world.

Recitation: *How Flowers Grow (38)*

This new life makes people glad, it makes the world look glad.

Recitation: *'Tis God Who Sends the Spring (39)*

LEADER: Springtime tells us a greater story than new life in flowers and trees. It tells the Easter story.

Recitation: *Easter (40)*

LEADER: Many things at Easter time help to tell the story. The fragrance of the lily bells. The glad song of the church bells. The happy voices of the children join the great Easter chorus—Christ is risen.

Prayer: *An Easter Prayer (41)*

MOTHER'S DAY

On Mother's Day we celebrate
And recognize our Mother,
Showing her how much we care
For her above all others.

Thanking her for all she does,
And giving her our praise.
Telling her the things
We may forget on other days.

—Jackie Wilson

FOR MY MOTHER

Dear God, I love my mother,
But, I find it hard to say
The words that tell my love for her
Upon this Mother's Day.

If I'm afraid or I get hurt
She hears me when I call;
She loves me so, and understands
My problems—one and all!

Oh, thank you God, for all she does,
Her love and care for me;
Please tell her heart the lovely things,
I whisper now, to thee.

—Arletta Christman Harvey

A MOTHER'S DAY CELEBRATION

(To be used within a worship service)
Litany of Praise *(Paraphrased from the Proverbs of Solomon)*

LEADER: The wise woman builds her house and walks uprightly in the love of the Lord. In the Lord, her children find refuge.

PEOPLE: The Lord is high above all nations and the Lord's glory is above the heavens. The Lord gives a woman her home, making her the joyous mother of children.

LEADER: We must hear then, our Father's commandments and listen to our Mother's teachings.

PEOPLE: They shall be as a fine garland for our head and a pendant for our neck.

LEADER: The Lord's commandment is a lamp, and the Lord's teaching a light, wise instruction for all who will learn.

PEOPLE: When we walk, this knowledge will lead us, and when we rest it will watch over us. God has richly blessed us, and we will rejoice!

ALL: Glory be to the Father, and to the Son and to the Holy Spirit. Amen.

Reading: THE LOVE OF GOD

Like a cradle, rocking, rocking,
　　Silent, peaceful, to and fro,
Like a mother's sweet looks dropping
　　On the little face below,
Hangs the green earth, swinging, turning,
　　Jarless, noiseless, safe and slow;
Falls the light of God's face; bending
　　Down and watching us below.

And as feeble babes that suffer,
　　Toss and cry, and will not rest,
Are the ones the tender mother
　　Holds the closest, loves the best;

So when we are weak and wretched,
    By our sins weighed down, distressed,
Then it is that God's great patience
    Holds us closest, loves us best.

O great Heart of God! whose loving
    Cannot hindered be nor crossed;
Will not weary, will not even
    In our death itself be lost—
Love divine! of such great loving
    Only mothers know the cost,
    Cost of love, which all love passing,
    Gave a Son to save the lost.   —*Saxe Holm*

Hymn: FAITH OF OUR MOTHERS *(Common Meter 8686)*

The faith of mothers everywhere
We celebrate today.
We learned from them to love the Lord,
To thank and praise and pray.

Young Samuel from his mother's hand
Was giv'n to old Eli.
When God, the Father, spoke to him,
He answered, "Here am I."

And Mary took her tiny Babe
For blessing from above.
The temple law proscribed the price—
A pair of turtle doves.

Dear Lord, we ask a blessing now
For Mothers, for us, too,
That we may all our faith renew
And pledge our lives to you.   —*Barbara W. Nordin*

Recitation: *Mother's Day (44)*

Hymn: *Happy the Home*

Recitation: *For My Mother (44)*

ROBIN

(First child)   God sent a Robin
Here today
To tell us summer's
On its way.

(Second child) Robin stopped and
Said hello
Just so everyone
Would know.   *—Jackie Wilson*

MY FATHER

I'll treat my father special
Give him lots of love today,
To let him know how much I care
For him in every way.

I'll give him hugs and kisses
And I'll shower him with praise,
To thank him for his patience
As he teaches me God's ways.

I'll wish him happy Father's Day
And smile from ear to ear,
And give him all the love I have
For Father's Day this year.

—Jackie Wilson

FATHER'S DAY

(First child)
> Kids need their dads
> Most every day
> To teach them how
> To work and play.

(Second child)
> They need their dad
> To throw a ball
> And pick them up
> If they should fall.

(Third child)
> Dads are good at
> Lots of things,
> Like fixing bikes
> And broken swings;

(Fourth child)
> Teaching kids to help their mother
> Love their sister
> And their brother.

(Fifth child)
> But the thing
> A Dad does best
> Is hug you tight
> Against his chest.

(All)
> God made daddys
> Special this way
> That's why we celebrate
> Father's Day!

—Jackie Wilson

HAPPY FATHER'S DAY

Happy, happy
Father's Day
To all the
Fathers here.

Let's make each day
Be Father's Day
Throughout the
Coming year!

—*Jackie Wilson*

FOR SUNSHINE AND FLOWERS

For sunshine warm and kind,
For flowers that I find
Out in my yard,
For pretty stones and birds that sing,
For soft, green grass and everything,
Father, I thank you.

—*Arletta Christman Harvey*

INDEPENDENCE DAY

Flags and banners
Everywhere
Red, white, and blue
Fly in the air.

Independence Day
Is here.
We celebrate
Once every year,

Our freedom won
By soldiers brave;
On battlefields
Their lives they gave.

Freedom lets us
Run and play,
To work and not
Worry what we say.

Freedom lets us
Sing and pray,
And worship God
In our own way.

Thank you, God,
For freedom won
Through lives freely given
Like your only son.

—Jackie Wilson

A PRAYER FOR OUR NATION

God bless our nation
Brave and strong.
Grant us peace
For which we long.

Guide our leaders.
Keep them strong.
Help our country
Do no wrong.

Show us daily
Your true way.
For all these gifts
Dear Lord God we pray.

Amen.

—*Jackie Wilson*

AUTUMN

Apples mellow,
Pumpkins yellow,
Tell the time of year;
Nuts are falling,
Nature calling,
Autumn time is here.

Colors gaily,
Changing daily,
Brighten field and wood;
Autumn's glory
Tells the story,
God is great and good.

—Ida F. Leyda

GRATITUDE

I thank You for these gifts, dear God,
    Upon Thanksgiving Day—
For love and laughter and the faith
    That makes me kneel to pray.

For life that lends me happiness,
    And sleep that gives me rest,
These are the gifts that keep my heart
    Serene within my breast.

Love, laughter, faith and life and sleep,
    We own them, every one—
They carry us along the road
    That leads from sun to sun.

—Margaret E. Sangster

FALL

God changed the world
While I slept last night
Painted the leaves
With colors so bright.

Painted them red,
Orange, yellow and brown;
Giving each tree its
Own colorful crown.

Soon the leaves will
Come tumbling down
Making a carpet
To cover the ground.

God's beauty surrounds us
Everyday
In trees and flowers
And birds at play.

God's beauty reminds
Us clear and true
God's love is real
For me and for you.

—Jackie Wilson

THANKSGIVING

We celebrate a holiday
At this time every year,
When we express our thankfulness
For all that we hold dear.

Thanksgiving brings all kinds of folks
Together to break bread.
They pause and bow their solemn heads
As thankful prayers are said.

—Jackie Wilson

THREE WINDOWS

Hope

In God lies hope
In times of strife;
That we might live
Christ gave his life.

Priorities

We build the house
In which we live;
To God on high
Our thanks we give.

Worship

With thankfulness
Let us give praise
To God who guides us
All our days.

—Merle Ray Beckwith

FROM THANKSGIVING

From Thanksgiving we capture a fellowship sweet
That lasts until the rest of this year is complete.
For rich harvest has ripened all throughout the land,
And our lives are enriched as we trust in God's hand.

While the world is a festering with wounds that are done
At the time of Thanksgiving let our course be run
To give thanks for the efforts in tilling the plow
And before God our Maker to earnestly bow.

Come oh come all you people throughout our dear land
Come let's gather together each one hand in hand.
Thanks for turkey and dressing and sweet pumpkin pie.
Praise to God in the firmament on high.

—Merle Ray Beckwith

A PRAYER

Loving God, hear your little children
While to you we pray.
Asking for your loving blessing
On this happy day.

—Alice Jackson
paraphrased

MOTION PRAYER

(All)

We fold our hands that we may be
From earthly play and work set free;
We bow our heads as we draw near
The King of kings, our Father dear;
We close our eyes, that we may see
Nothing to take our thoughts from thee.
Into our hearts we pray you will come,
And may they each become your home;
This is our prayer we bring to thee.
Then open our eyes, your light to see,
Lift up our heads to praise you still,
Open our hands to do your will.

Amen.

FATHER, WE THANK THEE

(First child)

> For flowers that bloom about our feet,
> For tender grass so fresh and sweet,

(Second child)

> For song of bird and hum of bee,
> For all things fair we hear or see,

(Third child)

> For blue of stream and blue of sky,
> For pleasant shade of branches high,

(Fourth child)

> For fragrant air and cooling breeze,
> For beauty of the blooming trees,

(Fifth child)

> For mother-love and father-care.
> For brothers strong and sister fair,

(Sixth child)

> For love at home and here each day,
> For guidance lest we go astray,

(Seventh child)

> For this new morning with its light,
> For rest and shelter of the night,

(Eighth child)

> For health and food, for love and friends,
> For everything Thy goodness sends,

(All)

> Father in heaven, we thank Thee.

—*Ralph Waldo Emerson*

A PRAYER BEFORE READING THE BIBLE

And now we take your holy book,
　The Bible, in our hand;
We listen for your word to us,
　And try to understand.

—Richard H. Bennett

A PRAYER BEFORE SINGING

Dear Father, listen while we sing
　Our happy song to you;
It tells you that we love you,
　And we know you love us, too.

—Richard H. Bennett

PRAYER FOR SUNDAY SCHOOL

For this day of new beginnings,
For my friends, our fun and play,
For the teachers as they guide me
In the learning of this day.

For your care that guards me always,
For the love that holds me true;
Keep me now, dear Heavenly Lord,
At my best the whole day through. Amen.

—Arletta Christmas Harvey

WHEN WE'RE HAPPY AT OUR PLAY

(First child)
> Dear God, because you're everywhere,
> We do not always kneel to pray;
> You hear our words of thankfulness
> While we are at our play!

(Second child)
> You know the gladness in our hearts;
> You love to see us work and play;
> And you will watch o'er all we do
> Throughout each happy day!

(All)

> Thank you, dear God, for happiness,
> And while we play, be near to bless.

—*Arletta Christman Harvey*

PRAYER

Teach me, my God and King,
In all things thee to see,
And what I do in anything,
To do it as for Thee. Amen.

—*George Herbert*

BE WITH US

The Lord be with us as we walk
Along our homeward road;
In silent thought or friendly talk,
Our hearts be near to God.

—*John Ellerton*

58

LORD, HEAR OUR PRAYER

(This prayer is suitable for several young children and one older child who will say the longer verse and lead the others in the part they say together.)

(First child)

Dear Lord, in you we put our trust,
Knowing that you are always just.

(All)

Lord, hear our prayer.

(Second child)

We ask to be all your own,
Living for you alone.

(All)

Lord, hear our prayer.

(Third child)

Our lives in your care
With gladness we place,
Your plan for each one,
O help us to trace.
With joy in our hearts
The future we face.

(All)

Lord, hear our prayer. Amen.

—Anonymous (Adapted)

THANK YOU, GOD

I thank you Lord for Mom and Dad
My home and all my friends,
My Sunday School and church and all
The blessings that you send.

—Jackie Wilson

GOD IN HEAVEN, BLESS ALL CHILDREN

God in heaven, bless all children;
Keep us always in your care;
May we know you, love and serve you;
All the children everywhere.

—Ida F. Leyda
(adapted)

THANK YOU

We have so much to thank you for,
Our heavenly Father dear,
For life and love and tender care,
Through all the happy year.

For homes and friends and daily food,
Each one a gift of love;
For every good and perfect gift
Is from our Lord above.

—Ida F. Leyda

GIVING

We like to give to those we love,
And so we bring to thee
Our precious gifts, and leave them here,
Dear Lord, for you to see.

—Richard H. Bennett

PARTING PRAYER

Jesus, Savior, give your blessing,
Keep us in your tender care, now as we part
May we be loving to one another,
May your love fill every heart.

A SERVICE FOR RALLY DAY

Prelude

Call to worship

LEADER: O God, open our lips.

PEOPLE: And our mouths shall show forth your praise.

ALL: Praise the Lord!

Hymn of Praise: *All Hail the Power of Jesus' Name*

Invocation

(In unison)
O God, grant that we may love you with all our heart, with all our mind and with all our strength. Help us to always love our neighbors and to live at peace with all people. Cleanse our hearts of envy, impatience, and ill will. Fill us with kindness and compassion that we may rejoice in the happiness and success of others and share with them in their sorrows. So may we live and work together as your children in the spirit of Jesus Christ our Lord. Amen.

Recitation: *Prayer for Sunday School (57)*

The Lord's Prayer

Recitation: *A Prayer Before Reading the Bible (57)*

Scripture Lesson: Acts 2:1-7, 16-17

Pastoral Prayer

Recitation: *Giving (60)*

Offering

Doxology

Sermon

Litany of Dedication
LEADER: God formed us from the dust of the ground and

breathed into us the breath of life; and we became living souls.

PEOPLE: You made us for yourself, O God, and our hearts are restless until they rest in you.

LEADER: God made the world and to all things in it; God made from one all the nations of people to dwell on the face of the earth.

PEOPLE: We thank you, O God.

LEADER: For the fresh revelation of yourself in each little child, and for the bonds of love which bind childhood, youth, and maturity together

PEOPLE: We thank you, O God.

LEADER: Jesus looked around at those seated about him and said, "Behold my mother and my family! Whoever does the will of God is my brother, my sister, my mother and my father."

PEOPLE: That belonging to one family is so clearly shown in the Scriptures and in the life of your Son—we thank you, O God.

ALL: We dedicate ourselves once again to you, O Lord. We consecrate ourselves gladly to teach and willingly to learn the Way, the truth, and the Life, that your whole family may be redeemed through Jesus Christ. Amen.

Hymn: *God Is So Good*

Benediction

A SERVICE FOR PROMOTION DAY

Prelude

Hymn: *We Are One in the Spirit*

Call to worship:

LEADER: O come, let us worship together!

PEOPLE: Let us kneel before our Lord!

Song *(by Preschoolers) "Jesus Loves Me"*

Recitation: *Welcome to our Sunday School (5)*

Promotion of Preschoolers

Song *(by youth choir) Pass It On*

Unison reading *(by children from middle grades) Psalm 100*

Promotion of Younger and Middle Elementary Departments

Recitation: *My Daily Creed (12)*

Recitation: *Jesus and the Children (23)*

Promotion of Older Elementary Children

Pastoral Prayer

Lord's Prayer

Offering

Recitation:: *Lord, When to You a Little Lad (21)*

Scripture reading *(by a young person) Acts 2:1-7, 16-17*

Hymn: *The Wise May Bring Their Learning*

Benediction